I0829025

A REVIEW

OF THE

"GREAT" SPEECH

OF

SENATOR JOHN P. JONES,

ON THE

BANKING AND CURRENCY BILL,

DELIVERED IN THE

UNITED STATES SENATE,

April 1st, 1874.

BY HENRY S. FITCH,

SAN FRANCISCO.

EDWARD BOSQUI & CO., PRINTERS, CORNER CLAY AND LEIDESDORFF STREETS.

1875.

A REVIEW OF

SENATOR JONES' SPEECH.

BY HENRY S. FITCH.

The specious speech of Senator Jones during the discussion on what is called the Banking and Currency Bill, has created a decided sensation all over the country. Upon what foundation, and rational argument, this examination may help to determine.

It is claimed by the friends of Mr. Jones, to have been delivered "on the spur of the moment." I do not propose to contend against the potential attributes of the Deity nor demur to the influences ascribed to the *gentleman in black;* but, if the claim of his friends is made for the purpose of disarming a critical examination into its truthful merits, I am keen to declare that I have no respect for the "spur of the moment." I will however deal, with the gentlest consideration for Mr. Jones' feelings, and not too rudely attempt to shake the exalted estimation in which he is held.

In the excitement of a first perusal of Mr. Jones' speech, the conclusion arrived at was, that about one hundred mistaken statements of fact, illogical deductions and untenable assumptions appeared. A subsequent and more careful examination has convinced me that my first estimate was greatly underrated.

In his debate on April 1st in the Senate on banking and currency, Senate bill No. 617 being under consideration, Senator Morton said:

Mr. President, what is the use of talking about gold when you have not got it? The Senator from Ohio in all this session has never attempted to tell us how we can resume specie payments. The whole world knows we have not got the gold. The country is in the condition of a man who is rich, who has got a great deal of valuable property, who is in a fine condition, but has not the money. He has got that which is worth the money many times over, but has not got the money. We have got the country—the country is prosperous, but the gold is not in the country, and everybody knows it, and yet we hear gold talked about here.

Mr. JONES—Will the Senator allow me to ask him a question?

Mr. MORTON—Yes, sir.

Mr. JONES—I should like to ask the Senator how it is that the State of Texas, the State of Oregon, the State of California and the State of Nevada, with less resources than most of the States of which he speaks, find no difficulty in having plenty of gold?

Mr. MORTON—So far as Texas is concerned, I am not so well advised about the condition of that State; but I can say in regard to California and Nevada, that I believe their banks from the very first declined to receive the legal tender currency in that country. California has shut it out, and it is the greatest blunder she has made. It has stood in the way of her prosperity all the time. California is a mining State, and Nevada, I believe, is almost exclusively a mining State, and when they insist that the currency of the country shall be gold, my answer is that it is to make the currency that which California and Nevada produce.

Mr. Jones' statement that the states referred to find no difficulty in having plenty of gold, is not true. *The rate of interest is the measure of abundance,* and every man must admit that where money commands from 12 to 60 per cent. per annum interest, it cannot be abundant.

Mr. Morton was as much deceived by the statement as he was mistaken in attempting to account for what was untrue

Mr. JONES—If the Senator will excuse me, the question I asked was how it was that those States, with less values of wheat and other such things to sell, can get the gold—a large amount of it—and retain it?

They do not retain it in large quantity; with the farmers and other industrial pursuits, the years' end finds them without money, save in exceptional instances. They cannot acquire gold in "large amount." If they did, some part of it, would be saved to them over their expenses, and they would not be obliged to borrow at the high rates of interest charged. The Senator says:

When the miners dig the gold they do not give it away.

Profundity, amazing! What do they do with it? Ah!

The people have to buy it, and buy it with something. And how do they retain the gold, being such poor States?

This is a conundrum which the able Senator should have answered. The miners dig gold and sell it to the bankers and their agents for coin, and use that coin in the purchase of, *not the luxaries,* but the necessaries of life—if we are permitted to except Senator Jones and a few like him, who seem in these days the especial favorites of the gods. But we will proceed with the colloquy:

Mr. MORTON—Gold is the product of Nevada. That is what the people go to Nevada for chiefly, and I believe it has been the policy of the financial men of Nevada to exclude greenbacks from the State, and it has been a blunder, in my opinion. Nevada only had 42,000 population in 1870; very few more, I think, than she had six or seven years before, and the probability is that she has got but few more now. She has got gold in abundance; her mountains are full of gold and silver, but she lacks people and she lacks prosperity.

Mr. Morton's rejoinder is only partially right. Nevada has mountains full of gold and silver, but her 42,000 population have not gold in abundant supply. For if they had, they would be prosperous, and the people of the world would find them out and immigrate thither.

No! The people of Nevada are energetic and industrious, but poor, as a class, and do not illustrate a prosperity very tempting to immigration.

WHY CERTAIN STATES LACK PROSPERITY.

Mr. Jones said:

Mr. President: It seems to me it is in the Middle States, the Western States, and the Southern States that lacks prosperity, when they come here and tell us they have no product with which they can get the kind of money that the world uses to transact their business with, and which is acknowledged everywhere to be the standard of value.

Another mistake! The Middle, Western, and Southern States, ask for a greater supply of the money of the Government, and complain because it is denied them, well knowing that the coin of the country cannot for a long time be supplied to them, answering to their needs. Again, they do not say, "they have no product with which they can get the kind of money the world uses," etc. For them to admit so much, would be an admission that they were without products to exchange for any kind of money—which is not true. Mr. Jones says:

I cannot see how it is that the currency of this country is at from 10 to 15 per cent. discount, and yet that there is not enough of it, unless it is because the people distrust their Government and have no faith in its stability.

The logic of this extract is, perhaps, as significant as any we shall find of the statesmanlike attainments of the author. He seems not yet to have learned that gold commands a premium, not for circulation in the Eastern States, where the paper money of the Government is at par—but for export—to meet the foreign demands on a small part of our people.

If Mr. Jones had not risen above his common sense, he would have discovered that his speech was in opposition to a bill before Congress asking for more of the money, which he affects to despise, and not appealing for gold at all; and, that if the people distrusted the faith and stability of the Government, their common sense would deter them from making the appeal. He says:

I presume that gold will travel to any country where it is not made a fugitive by vicious enactments that make irredeemable paper a legal tender for obligations and debts.

If gold is made a fugitive, by the vicious enactments of Congress, whereby "legal tenders" become acceptable to the people of the Eastern States, how shall the exodus of gold from the Pacific States be explained, and where Mr. Jones especially well knows, such enactments are not in force?

And why does not gold *travel* toward *us*, who are in the west, in view of the "vicious enactments" complained of? In California, by an act of its Legislature, the National Currency was repudiated, and thereby according to the logic of Senator Jones, there should be a redundancy of gold! The sober fact is proven that a sum in gold and silver, equal to our production becomes a fugitive from these shores every year. Surely Senator Jones either misunderstands his position, or he misapplies his principle. He says:

Whenever you make a paper money that has no intrinsic value whatever a legal-tender for the payment of debts, then gold will disappear from the circulation.

An assumption which he may find it difficult to prove. Since there is a difference of opinion touching the value of legal tenders, and other apparent causes for the disappearance of gold. The quotation is doubtless an illusion, which a little reflection will dispel.

"MR. MORTON—I asked him what would become of our country if all the States of the Union had followed the example of Nevada and rejected the legal-tenders?

MR. JONES—We should have put down the Rebellion for fifteen hundred millions less money than it did cost.

MR. HAMILTON, of Maryland—That is true."

An assumption, without justification, without dignity, and ridiculous for its exageration; an assurance, intolerable for its immodesty; insupportable for its extravagance; and insufferable for its egotism.

A declaration, impudent, as it was insulting to the Government; detestable in its taste, as it was discourteous to the Senate; defiant of reason, as it was disloyal and degrading.

The vigorous ebullition of Senator Hamilton in response to the declaration of Senator Jones, indicated the appreciation of the mortal blow that had been dealt to the loyal republican element of the country, and showed how *happily* "on the spur of the moment" our Republican Senator from Nevada, had stabbed the saviours of the nation, to the infinite satisfaction of traitors and known enemies of the Government.

Before the year shall end, we may be able to estimate the effect of this detestable insinuation.

MR. JONES.—That is what would have happened to this country. And more than this, as we should have been spared all the embarrassments and uncertainties which have nearly overwhelmed us during the past nine years.

The embarrassments and uncertainties are not perceptible, to which the Hon. Senator refers, unless it be those which attache to the administration of a Government, which had survived its great trial, put down the Rebellion, and won for itself the confidence and support of the loyal masses of the people.

We should have saved since the close of the war a hundred millions a year, and prevented untold disasters yet to come if we do not retrace our steps, and which will, as I believe, imperil the honor and prosperity of the country.

The Hon. Senator, makes another declaration denunciatory of the Government, and which in no sense refers to the monetary enactments before Congress, as shown in the above ambiguous extract.

He does not show, *in what manner* one hundred millions per annum could have been saved since the close of the war, nor is he able to show such a result, as depending upon any financial action of the Nation. Senator Jones, *as a Senator*, should understand for what the one hundred millions has gone from the country, and by what Congressional device, it could have been retained, and if he has the power and intelligence which his assumptions would imply, state for the benefit of the Nation, not only the errors of the past, but, the measures calculated to retrieve us from our losses, if any there be. "It is the province of greatness *to bid to something*." Why so reticent of what should be done, and so liberal in denunciation of what *has been done?*

His reference to untold disasters yet to come, and the prophetic implication born of such unsubstantial vagaries, is as unbecoming as it is unsuited to the Senatorial toga.

Senator Jones continues, "Why, Sir, if the opportunity the war gave us to issue the greenbacks had been denied us, and if such great benefits, as some seem to think, have flowed from such issue, I tremble at the contemplation of the condition we should have been in if peace had continued, and the glorious opening had been lost to us forever; for with the increase of population and the alleged necessity of a certain amount of money *per capita*, we never could have owed enough on which to do our business."

I am at a loss to determine, whether the last quotation of the Hon. Senator, was an unsuccessful attempt at sarcasm, or an overdrawn figure of speech, intended to wring applause from his hearers, for its unintelligibility.

Senator Jones says: "Now, Sir, what did happen? Ignoring the history of other nations; taking no warning from the wrecks of false financial systems strewn along their pathway, the first thing we did was to make irredeemable paper a legal tender, and thereby almost immediately advanced the price of everything one hundred per cent."

Senator Jones, unfortunately for himself, ignores the history of the time he refers to. The Government had already made a loan from the Eastern banks, a second loan had been applied for, by the Government, and was supplied on terms which were disgraceful in loyal citizens to demand.

The loyal men at the head of the Government sought a remedy from the financial pressure, so rapidly accumulating, by application to the country which gave the Hon. Senator birth, (and from where he, has doubtless imbibed much of his Anglo-American liberality,) without obtaining the necessary financial aid. England and France had a bone to pick with America upon the subject of the "Monroe doctrine." A strong hold upon the Earth's chess board, engaged their especial attention, and it was *impolitic* for England to afford monetary assistance to a nation, which stood in her way, and had shown a disposition to oppose her in her acquisition of territory upon this continent. Senator Jones, if he were an American in heart, should have known when he uttered such anti-American sentiments in the Senate of his adopted country, that the *legal tender* was the only resource left to the nation, whereby the war could be carried on, and the maintenance of the Government made possible.

The doubling of prices, which the Hon. Senator places so much stress upon, was attained before the issue of the legal tenders, as he may readily learn. The audacity of proclaiming against a measure, which the loyal sentiment of the country approved—which was recommended by such men as Lincoln, Stanton and Chase, and a host of other patriotic and noble men, at that time in the administration of the Government, is so uncalled for, and so vicious, that those southern chiefs against whom the nation were once at war, may well discover in Senator Jones the gifted exponent of their hate.

Senator Jones, "Having thus made everything we were compelled to buy double its former price, we then entered upon the negotiation of loans, and a rigorous system of taxation to raise money with which to buy. This we should have done in the start, and what we could have done; but we first thoroughly demoralized the whole country and all its industries; we plundered the creditors and allowed the debtors to discharge their obligations by paying from 30 to 50 per cent."

Does Senator Jones suppose, that only he, of all the people of this Nation understood the status of affairs? In the crisis of a great war, bearing heavily upon the country, are there any but the disloyal through all time, who have the affrontery to charge those in Congress at that period with unmindfulness of the highest interests of the people?

The policy of taxation was well discussed, and it was found, that there was not money enough in the Country to pay the taxes, if assessed in a sum equal to the necessities of the war. The taxes were increased gradually as the means of paying them were added by the Government, and Senator Jones should know better than to declare that a demoralization of the industries of the country existed during that unhappy period, save by the demands the Government made for men to prosecute it.

No man was enabled to make the percentage on the payment of his debt, as the Senator states, save those who lived on this coast, and who availing themselves of a repudiated currency, profited by selling their gold, and paying their debts in the East, where it was loyally received at par, more to the credit of the East than to the West, at this time so remarkably represented. He says:

We resorted at the outset to measures condemned by financiers everywhere.

Assumption is cheap! Who were the financiers, that condemned these financial measures of the Government? If we except a few New York bankers, and that faction, who wept over our victories, and shouted joyfully over our defeats, we know them not—possibly the Hon. Senator may refer to financiers of Great Britain! He says:

A great war cannot be carried on by pieces of paper payable at convenience and bearing no interest.

What will the Hon. Senator do with the *fact that it was* so carried on? much as he may regret it. Senator Jones says:

This paper currency, instead of adding strength to the imperiled country, was a source of weakness. Its issuance was an impeachment of the patriotism of the nation, and an underrating of the resources of the country. It was a cheat upon the people in teaching them the pernicious idea that, in carrying on a great civil war, economy and industry were not necessary; that production and destruction were convertible terms.

Another ridiculous assumption. The country was strengthened, as experience has well proved. Without the beneficent provision of the currency, the country was weak—with it, was it made strong, and the results following its introduction are the proofs of it.

The adoption and acceptance of the National Currency by all the states, save one or two, is a matter of history which, even Senator Jones cannot revise to suit his will. What States impeached the patriotism of the Nation? Those who warmly and loyally accepted it? or those who rejected it?

What part of the Country pronounced the legal tenders a cheat upon the people, but that part of the people whom the Hon. Senator so ably represents?

Can economy and industry only be taught through deprivation and want? Are production and destruction made convertible terms by the wise enactments of a free Republican Government?

But Senator Jones' speech is long, and I must be brief. He says:

Much is said about the value of the greenback; the superior quali ty of the Goverment money, the best, they tell us, that the world has ever seen; one Senator, in a moment of supreme exaltation, declaring it "battle-born." We are told that the honor and entire resources of this great Government are pledged to its redemption. What is this "great Government" so far as that pledge is concerned? At present it is in this Senate.

It must have furnished an impressive scene in the Senate of the United States, when the angular Anglo-American Senator from the State of Nevada, asked the Senate, "what is this great Government," so far as its pledges are concerned?

The assumption that the Senate of which the Hon. gentleman is a member, "is at present the Government," is a conceit, which it may require the whole term for which he has been elected to eradicate from his mind. Senator Jones continues:

Some appear to think that there is a power exclusive of this body whose honor is pledged to the redemption of the greenbacks. If this Senate votes that it will not pay them, then the honor of the country is not pledged at this time to their redemption.

The Senator had forgotten, that the subject of redemption of the Government greenbacks was not before the House, a bill on quite another subject was under consideration, why did he not wait until a bill came up for consideration, having for its object, the provisional means, to redeem the Government currency, and then, "on the spur of the moment," and without preparation, instruct the Senate in regard to its powers, and the ease with which its action could relieve the nation from responsibility, in regard to redemption?

Mr. LOGAN—The Senator spoke of the pledge of this Senate representing the Government. He does not mean to say that the Senate is the Government?

Mr. JONES—So far as the redemption of the Government's promises are concerned it is.

Mr. LOGAN—Then every time the Senator is defeated a part of the Government is defeated.

Mr. JONES—Of course. I mean that the Senate is the Government, not in its power to enact a law, but in its power to prevent the enactment of one. No law can be passed without the assent of the Senate. When Senators grow eloquent about some great government, so sacred that we scarcely dare to raise our eyes and gaze upon it, being pledged to the redemption of these pieces of paper, what do they mean? Do they not know that whenever a majority of this body refuses to vote that this paper shall at some future time be redeemed, then that pledge is broken and the honor on which it rested is scattered to the four winds and vanishes into thin air?

If the Senator is to believed, "*some*" great government was pledged to "redemption of these pieces of paper." The question asked of the Senate, "what do they mean," would naturally be answered, *that they mean what they say.* The attempt of Senator Jones to awaken the apprehension of the people, concerning the responsibility of the Government for their ultimate redemption, by the assertion that a vote of the majority of the Senate would necessarily put it beyond the power of the Government to redeem, is as unworthy of him as it was illogical and untimely. Surely, our new Senator must have been drawn into a discussion upon a subject for which he was unprepared, and altogether *upon the spur of the moment.*

In 1870 there were about two million of people engaged in manufactures. They received about $775,000,000 in wages. In other words, about 50 per per cent. more were engaged in the business of manufactures than in 1860, and they received about double the wages.

If Senator Jones is right in his statistics, the showing of an increase of 50 per cent. of laboring arms employed, and a double increase of wages, is of itself an argument in favor the Government currency that all his sophistries cannot overturn.

If he be a friend to the industrial interests of the country, why does he proclaim against a measure which has served them so well?

The capital used in this manufacturing business was about $2,100,000,000. One would suppose that the product would be about 50 per cent., certainly not more than 75 per cent. above that of 1860; but the product, instead of being $1,800,000,000, was $4,200,000,000, or nearly 150 per cent. more than in 1860. This increase was in the price of the product and not the quantities produced.

There is nothing in *this statement* to prove that the national currency had anything to do with the price put upon the products by the manufacturer. It may have enabled the manufacturer to enlarge his works, and pay a larger roll of labor. The manufacturer may over-estimate the commercial demand—a mistake not unfrequently made by the very best men.

But, the explanation which Senator Jones makes to illustrate his theory, utterly confounds his argument. He says:

These figures seemed to show extraordinary prosperity in the manufacturing interests; but the panic of September dispelled the illusion. The tremendous superstructure of credit upon which this apparent prosperity rested was based on too slender a foundation of actual capital, and the moment public confidence was shaken, the entire manufacturing interests of the country were paralyzed, and many of the oldest houses ruined.

He admits, that it was the superstructure of credit—not the National Credit, for that has stood unshaken; not the mistrust that greenbacks would never be redeemed, as he would have us believe, for that was unasked; not the plans which were being considered by Congress, for the Nation's benefit, for these encouraged the people—but the *individual, personal,* or *corporate,* responsibility and status of the manufacturers themselves. *That,* was the credit put in peril, not by any act of the Government, but by the strain which personal credit had put upon private responsibility.

I have seen the favorite mining stock which the Hon. Senator is said to hold by the ream (Crown Point) selling at *two dollars per share,* under what the Senator will understand to be a "*bear*" influence, but nobody, not even the embryotic Senator of that time, convinced it to be the fault of the Government!

I have seen the same stock rise from two dollars per share to two thousand dollars per share, but heard no voice of the Senator raised against the Government, on account of the enormous advance in value! Again have I seen it tumble, from two thousand dollars per share to seven hundred. I heard the howl of despair from those who were "long," and suffered loss, but never a whimper against the Government for having put greenbacks in circulation.

If the Senator's memory had been equal to his invention, he might have stated in his "masterly speech," that during the crisis referred to, legal tenders approximated nearly to the price of gold. Not more than three per cent. difference! Does that show the distrust of the people? If gold was in abundance, and sufficient to enable Congress to resume specie payment, why was it not used to relieve the people, in their hour of greatest need? It, too, was a a legal tender! and if, as Senator Jones asserts, *abundant,* why should the premium on gold recede to 6 per cent., whilst legal tenders stood at 4 per cent. premium, that is 4 per cent. above the par of National bank notes. The panic, and paralysis, seems occasioned more by the *want* of legal tenders, and their scarcity, than objection to them, as money.

The Superintendent of the Census computes the average increase in prices of manufactured articles at 56 per cent. in 1870 over those of 1860. The farmers and producers of our raw material pay this 56 per cent. upon all they consume in the production of their crops, and in addition thereto they pay enormous profits which the retail dealers always exact when an inconvertible paper currency is the circulating medium.

If the Hon. Senator, here refers, to the Census computations, it is proper I suppose, to ask if he deems them reliable, and if so, why he has declared elsewhere in his speech, that the increase in prices from 1860 to 1870, was 150 per cent.?

If figures don't lie, on whom shall we fix the "inaccuracy" of the statements made? There is quite a difference between 56, and 150 per cent.! We will seize upon the first and only authority, which the Senator has had the indiscretion to give, and suppose, that, the Superintendent of the Census, is correct, I am determined to be liberal, in this examination of the Senator's speech, and now with great satisfaction acknowledge, that, up to this point, I have found one statement only, which was logical, or true in any degree, and that blessed *one,* nearly 200 per cent. exaggerated.

The by-play with which, Senator Jones seeks to cajole the farmers and producers into the support and approval of his most extraordinary declamation, is too feeble an effort, to command attention at this time.

And now as to the condition of the agricultural interest in 1870. The decade between 1850 and 1860, exhibited a much higher deree of prosperity in this direction than that between 1860 and 1870, viewing it from whatever stand-point you choose. People seem to have left their farms and sought the cities to engage in the semi-gambling business of manufacturing, made so by an inconvertible paper money.

The grand effort of Senator Jones, which has so "electrified the country," has only to be examined in *pieces,* to enable this great nation to understand how small an electric apparatus, it requires, in these days of remarkable invention, to reach so far and to produce such startling effects.

It may be observed, that the diction of the Hon. Senator, is very frequently confused by his "inconvertible-paper-money" attachments, with which he fondly closes so many of his sentences. It suggests the idea, that a search for the sinister cause of his redundant antipathy may not be in vain, and if found, before bidding adieu to the Hon. Senator, he shall have the pleasure of seeing it presented with verbal illustrations.

To return to our task, we are shown in the search before us a sample of tremendous research. The Hon. Senator thinks, confidently, that, a much higher degree of prosperity, was exhibited in the Agricultural departments of the country during the decade between 1850 and 1860, than was manifested during the decade following!

Senator Jones, evidently refers to a period when the country was undivided, and if neither he, nor his friends object, I shall ask, *what of it*. (I will say, *en passant*, that, right here, Senator Jones, threw away an opportunity of exhibiting a statesmanlike quality if he had it to spare, which would have been worth more to him, than the defeat of the bill under consideration.) Between the years 1850 and 1860, the whole country was at peace, and the Agricultural interests of the nation were undisturbed, and checked only by a too limited supply of money. The years, between 1860 and 1870, are memorable to the American people, on account of a *four years war*, the most distressing and depleting, in its demand for material forces, to carry it on, (upon both sides) that has ever taxed a nation. Millions of men—in large part drawn from the Agricultural districts, and the peaceful fields of labor—to take part, in the battle field, very many thousands of them, to the great grief of the nation, never returning to take part again in the industrial pursuits of men.

Many thousands who did return to their homes, were so maimed and bruised, and battle worn, and sicklied by the plagues of war, that the scythe, nor the many useful implements of husbandry, were they able more to use.

Many sick, poor and despondent, willing to work for their precious lives in whatever ways they could, with honor.

To the poor and the needy, and the absolutely dependent, employment is a blessed boon.

Many of these soldier heroes, disabled by the terrific conflict, wished still to live, and sought to earn their bread and raiment by employing themselves, mutilated as they were, where employment could be given by the manufacturers.

The nation if for no other cause than this alone, should be thankful that the mechanical and manufacturing establishments were, by the beneficent provisions of the Government, upheld, sustained and still able to give employment to the laboring and necessitous.

That is the proper stand point from which to view this question, and that is the honorable view to take of it. Senator Jones to the contrary notwithstanding. If Senator Jones has not become so bedizened by his financial and political success, that he is lost to a comprehension, or even a passing recollection of the war, occuring in the decade he so dexterously arraigns, and the condition of the country since that melancholy period, he may find a cause for the condition he names without referring it to the inconvertible paper money he so contemptuously assails, or charge the worthy and enterprising manufacturers of the country with following an illegitimate pursuit, which the Hon. Senator inconsiderately stigmatizes as "semi-gambling."

The Hon. Senator, approaching the profound study of mathematics, should be heard :

In 1860 there were thirteen hundred thousand people engaged in manufactories in this country. The wages paid them amounted to about $378,000,000.

The capital stock of the manufacturing establishments of the United States was about $1,000,000,000, the product was $1,800,000,000, and I will say that during that year our exports were much larger than our imports. We were exporting of cotton fabrics about $12,000,000, I believe, to China,

It may be remembered that Senator Jones declared, that 2,000,000 people were engaged in manufacturing in 1870—an increase of 50 per cent. on the number employed, and at an advance of 100 per cent. on the wages paid for the year 1860. In 1860, $1,000,000,000 capital employed in manufactures, the product was $1,800,000,000.

In 1870, the same industry, with $2,000,000.000 capital produced $4,200,000,000, from which take cost of raw matertial $2,400,000,000, and the wages paid employees $775,000,000 and a result to the manufacturers is reduced to $1,799,225,000.

Now, if we take from this sum the shrinkage in the market value of the product upon the first sum of $4,200,000,000, as more or less of it was pushed to sale at or about the time of the panic, and we arrive at a solution of the question of manufacturers' profits, and make the profits of the agricultural producers appear amply satisfying by contrast.

The insinuations of Senator Jones of the enormous and most tempting profits of the manufacturer, is answered by the unmistakable ruin that has fallen upon them.

In this view of the case, it may be proper to ask Senator Jones, where he finds justification for his attempt to stigmatize the manufacturers of the country? And why it is, that he utters sentiments calculated to excite a prejudice against them, not only on the part of the agriculturists, but others who understand the term "gamblers," without the Hon. Senator's too free interpretation of it.

And where does the Hon. Senator find support for his limp and mistaken argument against the national currency? His references have thus far proved as damaging to his argument as his assumptions.

If the profits of manufacture did not reward the capital employed, certainly the labor employed and paid for, was a benefit to the country. Senator Jones proceeds:

And yet honorable Senators inform us here that we want more paper money, so that the inflation of personal property and of stocks, and of the business that draws our population to the cities, shall be indefinitely increased; that speculation shall be aggravated, and that the farmer shall receive less and less from year to year, while the gambler and the stock-jobber shall get more and more. They want money for what? I have seen nobody anywhere who wants to hire out, but everybody wants to hire somebody else.

Senator Jones has declared that there was no greater quantity of manufactures produced in 1870 than in 1860. If that be so, the materials drawn from agricultural sources must have been utilized at prices satisfactory to the producers, and that industry will not be likely to follow Mr. Jones in his denunciation of the national currency. By his own theory, the farmer is represented as receiving "less and less," whilst his own statements, examined, proves the fact that they receive "more and more"—a contradiction not at all rare with Senator Jones.

His allusion to the stock-jobbers and gamblers, and his queries of, "who wants money?" and his tirade against speculation, is simply *slovenly logic*, unbecoming a Senator of the United States.

What Senator Jones, wants, and what he don't want are indifferently stated by himself, in the following:

We do not want to have enterprise stimulated in this country. We want labor encouraged by better money. We want the laborer who receives his pay for a day's work to know that it will not shrink in value on his way to the store where he buys the necessaries of life.

If the Hon. Senator, don't want enterprise stimulated in this country, we may infer by parity of reason, that he wants to stimulate enterprise in *some other country*. It is a bold declaration for a Senator of the United States to make, because, it has been deemed, by the most civilized and progressive nations, to be sound policy, to encourage and stimulate enterprises, of every character, which would have a tendency to provide within themselves, as far as possible, not only the necessaries of life, but also the luxuries, required for home use and consumption, and as much as possible for export. The home policy of England for three quarters of a century, has been to encourage, and to stimulate by every means at the command of the Government, every enterprise which would tend to lessen her imports, and increase her exports. The country may not feel surprise, after this, if our Crown Point Statesman, takes an early occasion to announce himself the Champion of Free Trade.

He says "he wants labor encouraged by better money," and not liable to shrink in value, while on his way to the store. Senator Jones, should have announced, that this sentiment so artlessly appropriated as his own, was uttered by several public speakers in 1837, when General Jackson's pet banks, went to the dogs, and carried with them millions of the national deposits, and was intended as a rebuke to the Hero of New Orleans, for his veto of the United States Bank Bill, asking Congress for the extension of its charter, with which institution, the country had been served for twenty years; its bills never being at a discount, and very often commanding a premium, where exchanged for gold.

What Senator Jones says, about banks, may perhaps, repay the cost of re-print, not because it is a reliable reflex of his sentiments, but, because it is a rude embodiment of the expression of those who oppose all paper money.

We want no more banks of circulation without redemption, for though I admit they are great institutions for the accumulation of wealth, they do very little towards its production. They absorb nearly all the surplus property in their immediate vicinity. They adorn palatial residences the avenues where gamblers and stock-jobbers dwell, while they cover the farms with blisters in the shape of mortgages.

WHAT NEED OF MORE BANKS.

What relief can additional banks give to those who have no security to offer for loans? Who fails now to obtain loans on sufficient security? As it is claimed that there is but an insignificant profit of 2 per cent. on circulation, while money in the South and West commands from 1 to 2 per cent. a month, why are not banks of deposit, requiring no charter from Government, more to the purpose than additional banks of circulation? Will the money-lender refuse to be satisfied unless he receives not only interest on his capital, but also a charter from the Government to collect interest on what he owes? For the bank issues, which we call money, are really mere evidences of the bank's indebtedness.

Does the much eulogized bank currency lack the flexibility to enable it to reach the places where it is most wanted? Is the locality of the bank important to the borrower? Will not the best interest and securities bring the money from any distance for investment? If all the banks of the United States were in Texas, would New York suffer for the want of money? Did not the surplus capital of Europe come to carry on our war and build our railroads? Doubt that water will find its level; doubt that quicksilver will find the pores of the vessel containing it; doubt that atmosphere will press toward a vacum, but do not doubt that capital will seek the best investments as to interest and security.

I can see nothing to result from additional issues of inconvertible paper money but inevitable disaster. It would work the confiscation now of a small portion of the creditor's property for the use of the debtor, to be succeeded from time to time by further confiscations.

Most of the representatives here of States that are claimed to be debtor States desire an increase of this currency. I say to them that no nation can be strong and be dishonest; no nation can be strong and attempt to confiscate the property of one citizen and give it to another; no nation can make money plenty when it says to the creditor who has loaned it. "You shall receive back only a portion of what you have loaned in full satisfaction of the debt."

Were these reflections, made with a view to improve, by the substitution of some other device, the paper money of the country, the Hon. Senator's views would appear less objectionable. But in so far as it appears only aimed at the destruction of all paper money, we may safely rely upon its impotence and placidity to save us from mischief. Tame Hares do not invite our pursuit.

We will pass on to Senator Jones' grandiloquent *Apostrophe to Gold*, which reminds us of the serio-comic address of Horace Smith to the mummy.

Its diction feathers perceptibly of the abusive declamation of the fore part of this century. He says:

Gold is the articulation of commerce. It is the most potent agent of civilization. It is gold that has lifted the nations from barbarism. It has done more to organize society, to promote industry and insure its rewards, to inspire progress, to encourage science and the arts, than gunpowder, steam and electricity.

The use of gold had its origin in the necessities of mankind. The human heart is set upon it. It will command the proper services of everybody, at all times, and in all places. The necessities which compel its use are as inexorable to-day as they were at the beginning, although improved systems of exchange have diminished the proportionate volume necessary to do the work.

So exact a measure is it of human effort that, when it is exclusively used as money, it teaches the very habit of honesty. It neither deals in or tolerates false pretences. It cannot lie. It keeps its promises to rich and poor alike.

While it has seen human institutions perish and human governments crumble and decay, it is itself imperishable. The gold that was in Solomon's temple possessed the same qualities as the gold dug to-day from the sands of Africa. The gold of California and the gold of Australia are precisely the same. It defies the corroding hand of time and the friction of ages. It is the common denominator of values. It makes possible the classification of labor and the equitable interchange of commodities. Gold has represented the bargains made between men since the dawn of civilization, and it has never failed to faithfully fulfil its part as the universal agent and servant of mankind. But it withdraws from the companionship of the bedizened harlot called irredeemable paper money, and says to every people, "Banish her before you look for my return." It is the oxygen in the commercial atmosphere, and its absence produces financial asphyxia.

The value of gold is not affected by the stamp of the government. That is merely the final and reliable evidence of its weight and fineness.

You must have something with the attribute of extension, when you measure extension; to measure weight, you must have something of specific gravity; and to measure value, you must have something of value, something that requires labor to produce. Gold has this requisite. The stamp on a gold dollar says, in effect: "This government pledges its honor that this coin is nine-tenths fine, and contains 25.8 grains in weight." The government stamp on every piece of coin is a certificate to mankind that the bearer has rendered a service unto society, which is measured by that piece of metal, and that he is entitled to an equivalent service from society in return, payable on demand. Such a draft has never yet been dishonored.

What does a piece of this government paper say—this paper that the honor of the government is pledged to redeem, and which the custodians of that honor refuse to redeem, and refuse to take any steps toward redeeming? It says: "The holder of this piece of paper has rendered a service unto society, of an uncertain, unascertained, and unascertainable value, dependent entirely upon the precise day of the week or month when such service was rendered; and is entitled to such service in return as the 'bulls and bears' of Wall Street, or a vote of the Congress of the United States, or both, may determine." [Laughter.]

We are told that money is the utensil of trade; that it is the tool of the workman. Well, sir, it seems to me that our present currency, instead of being the spade of the husbandman, is the dice box of the gambler. [Applause.]

It is said that it is the grease that lubricates the wheels of commerce. Well, sir, it is a sort of grease that makes the hub expand, the spokes expand, and the axles expand. At one moment the grease spirts out on everybody, and the next this wheel without a tire is running dry on its axle. [Laughter.] Another difficulty is that the driver is too often diverted from the management of his wagon to speculation in the rise and fall of the grease.

England's opportunity to win and wear the world, *was lost* by such d—d vagaries as these.

The measure of the gold supply is understood. To rate the property of the world by this yellow god, has not half the consistency, of the worshipers of fire.

If as abundant as mankind could wish, its use would then be impracticable. To count, transfer, and convey the sums transacted in each day is simply impossible. To ignore the forms of paper money requisite in man's dealings, is neither less nor more than the harmless sneer of the senseless imbecile.

Confine ourselves to gold as a currency medium! It cannot be done by any civilized nation on earth, and there is no civilized nation who will attempt it. Forms of paper money must answer the demands and conveniences of trade. As well make requisitions on Milky Way for our daily rations, as to depend upon this yellow mummy with whom our Hon. Senator has become so infatuated.

Gold, is only in name, the articulation of commerce. Commerce languished until paper money came to its relief. Manufactures made but indifferent and uncertain progress till paper money came to its aid. Agriculture existed in demi-savage patches, until the world awakened under the influence of bills of public credit. The nations were unlifted from barbarism, till paper money made its appearance.

Society, was indifferently organized, industry uninspired, and progress only encouraged by the advent of a paper substitute for coin. Science and the arts lay sleeping, and gunpowder, steam and electricity, were unknown terms until, the discovery was made that paper money could answer to the call for gold.

The use of gold *had not* its origin in the *necessities* of mankind. It was its convenience, and interchangeable use, that recommended its adoption as money, and the same inducements apply to paper money to-day.

The human heart is not more set upon gold, than the paper money exchangeable for it, or the desired comforts which either can purchase. Good paper money commands the service of men as readily as gold, in all *civilized* countries.

The necessities which compel the use of paper money, are no less inexorable than those which call for gold, and the demand is equally answered by either. It is the improved systems which Senator Jones admits, that enables the world of action to be kept up, and added to, without the proportionate increase of the volume of gold.

These systems are in various degrees the improved devices, which make paper the equivalent for coin.

Paper money is as surely the measure of effort, as gold. It teaches *more* the habit of honesty, because credit is allied to honesty, and stimulated by it. Neither gold nor paper money deals in, or tolerates false pretences. Gold is gold, and no more; paper money is its representative and ally, good, if good—base, if base. If good, it keeps its promises and does not lie, to any, whilst gold has seen human goverments perish, paper money has been saved that humiliating sight. Paper money in all its vicissitudes, and through all its conflicts, has constituted the main-spring of human progress, and every civilized nation who have adopted it into their monetary systems, have made astounding progress, and those who have not, are tumbled into anarchy and retrogradation.

If gold possesses the magic and inherent principle of building up a nation, why does it cease to sustain them? What of Carthage, Troy, Rome, Jerusalem, and all other monuments of ancient grandeur, and all of the older nations who trod to the music of coined money? Of what certain sum in coin do they amount to now, in the light of a blessed civilization, unshackled by the restraint of coin, and the arbitrary classification of labor? Whatever is made by Government the vehicle of trade, the interchangeable specific of value, is now, and evermore will be, under an inspired civilization, recognized as money, whether it be gold or silver, or the paper money of the Government. Gold, the fixed meagre slave, inflexible, and unaccommodating to our needs;

paper, accommodating, flexible, and possessing the highest attributes of use for an active people, of what difference is it to men of action, if a ten dollar bill lack the specific gravity, only, of ten dollars in gold, the one of equal purchasing power with the other?

The assumption that the Government stamp, on either gold or paper, is to be regarded as a certificate of character, or offers any assurance of the honorable acquisition of it by the holder, is in keeping with many of the rhapsodies of the Hon. Senator, and no more entitled to respect than his ridiculous declamation, concerning the "Government paper," the "dice-box," the "gambler," the "lubricator," and other illuminated lollipops and sillibubs, with which he amused the Senate.

But why shall we continue at much greater length the examination of a speech whose author confines himself neither to the truths of history, nor to the known latitutes of fiction; who seems as likely to dress a hod carrier in the robes of State, as to bestow the charming features of a Venus upon a Satyr.

There are some specimens left of Senator Jones' style of argument. The following will repay perusal:

The money which consists of paper promises cannot be a standard of value. It measures nothing but the average hopes, fears, confidence, and doubts of this people as to the ability and intention of their Government to ultimately redeem it in gold, and is itself measured by gold. It finds its way into the pockets of speculators and gamblers, who win it, rather than the pockets of the laborers who earn it.

MR. MORTON—I will ask my friend a question. He talks about gambling. I will ask him if there has not been as much gambling in California and Nevada in the last ten or fifteen years as in any other State in the Union?

MR. JONES—The people there buy what they think is valuable and likely to increase in price, and if they have anything which they fear will fall in price they sell it. We have never had any money panics. We have never called upon the Congress of the United States to relieve the gambler from any portion of his liabilities, or to issue more money in order that he might more easily pay his debts.

Senator Jones seems not yet to have learned the powers of the Government. When it creates money, and stamps on its face the sum it shall represent, by *that act* is the standard of its value fixed.

Gold may command a premium. If it does, it rises above its standard. Greenbacks may do the same, or fall below its standard, the one no less variable than the other. It is generally understood that gold is treated as a commodity in all the Eastern States, and, for causes not mentioned by Senator Jones, commands a premium, whilst greenbacks pass for all commodities, even gold, at par. On the other hand, in California the standard value of gold is unaltered, and greenbacks are treated as a commodity, subject to a discount equivalent to the premium on gold in the East.

We have heard more objections raised by Senator Jones against greenbacks in his *one* speech, than have been said by the people since they were put in circulation.

Nobody doubts the ability of the Government to redeem its paper, in good time; but that is not at present the principal objection of the Senator. He says, "it gets into the pockets of the speculator and *gambler*, and not into the pockets f the laborer." Senator Jones seems to entertain a fearful prejudice against the speculator and *gambler*. It is to be hoped that a person of his incorruptible virtue has not suffered himself to be drawn into the den of the "tiger," and now resorts to the safe method of avenging his losses by the denunciations which so frequently crop out in his speech.

How Senator Jones should know the contents of a laborers pocket, cannot be properly authenticated, without his having *been there*, and his testimony of the *smartness* of the people of Nevada, whilst it may surprise them, "to a man," will not be considered a more extraordinary statement than that of never having any panics in California!

His final dash at the gamblers, and the evident stiffness with which he declares that the hated fraternity need not look to him for congres ional aid, would be amusing, if his style of argument was not already monotonous.

In the following quotation, it will be observed with satisfaction, on account of the variety it affords, that the Hon. Senator had substituted the "land-grabber" and speculator instead of the *gambler*—an improvement, indeed!

> We are told that our iron mills are idle. Well, sir, I hope they will remain idle until the men who labor in them can have better assurance of continuous employment and its reward than is furnished by the purchase of railroad iron on credit by bogus companies, which depend upon taxing the people to keep them up, or the sale of their bonds for funds with which to pay interest. If our mills are only to run spasmodically and overstock the market, or roll out iron for railroad tracks in uninhabited regions to enrich land-grabbers and speculators, I hope they will remain idle.

It is clear that neither hydraulic nor steam power is capable of forcing from the Hon. Senator any expression of sympathy for *iron mill owners*. Accounting for the late panic—he says:

> Those who had money hoarded it, instead of allowing its healthful circulation, and, as a consequence, stagnation, panic and ruin followed.

A money which the people so tenaciously hold and hoard, seems not a bad money to "tie to."

The affection of the people for greenbacks must have been spasmodic, or the Senator has missed his calculations:

> Suppose you vote $10,000 apiece to-day to every man in the country, what would be the result? The desire to borrow would cease when all were thus supplied, but about that time it would be discovered that the money was absolutely worthless, and the refrain of "more money" would change to the more sensible one of "better money."

The Hon. Senator strains his argument by supposing, what is not supposable, and "about that time" makes the important discovery, "that the money is absolutely worthless."

Well, if $10,000 apiece were voted to everybody, and it is found to be base, there is justification for the "refrain" of "more money" of better quality in place of it. The point which the Senator tried to make in the last paragraph must wiggle on in obscurity.

I hope the Senate will decide to stand by the integrity of the country. No government, no people, can be prosperous that ignores the proposition that honesty is the best policy; that, by any sort of legislation, disturbs the relationship between debtor and creditor; that tell the creditor that the hard day's work he has already performed and loaned to the debtor shall be repaid by half a day's work on the part of the latter; that attempts to "coin money in that false crucible called debt," and legalizes robbery by enacting that the base result shall be a legal tender.

The hope expressed by the Senator is refreshing; the instruction he volunteers, that "honesty is the best policy," addressing himself to the highest legislative body in the Government, by implication, insinuating, that he, the speaker, was *honest*, and those opposed to his views, *dishonest*, has in it a mixture of ill-bred audacity, only excelled by the impudence of his subsequent allegations that the Government were then about to enact, or ever had enacted, laws which legalizes robbery.

In the following paragraph we may find a key to the interest the Hon. Senator has in opposing the governmental substitute for gold:

THE PREMIUM ON GOLD NOT ENOUGH.

If money is scarce, I ask in the name of common sense, why will not people give more for it? Why do not the value of property in this country bear some just relation to the values of property all over the world? Why, sir, the premium on gold does not fully show the depreciation of this paper; and there is the difficulty. I differed from nearly every Senator on this floor in the reasons which induced me to support the amendment introduced by the Senator from New Jersey; [Mr. Frelinghuysen.] Objection was made by friends of that amendment that it would have a tendency to make gold rise in price. Now, sir, I say gold ought to rise. Every other commodity in this country—butchers' meat, groceries, provisions, and everything that enters into domestic use has risen, so that in relation to them greenbacks are really at a depreciation of fully 40 per cent. while in relation to gold, which has been shorn of its chief uses by being demonetized, the same greenbacks are at a depreciation of only 10 or 12 per cent. The effect of this is to discourage mining enterprise and depress mining interests. If the Government ever intends to resume specie payments those interests should be stimulated and encouraged by every legitimate means.

We had supposed, that a Senator of the United States, occupying the high position he does—elected to serve the people, rather than his own interests, would be a little slow to proclaim his belief, that a still wider difference should exist in the marketable rates at which gold should be exchanged for greenbacks, and not too boldly advocate the side which serves his individual interests; but, on the contrary, our expectation has been abused. The Hon. Senator takes the first occasion offered to proclaim his favor for that condition which serves with most profit his private interests.

In this unfortunate declaration of the Senator do we find the evidence of his unworthiness, and the mortifying reflection, that avarice has another ally to oppose such measures as should uphold the nation and conserve the public good. His concluding reference to the discouragement of mining enterprise, is too local in its application to be misunderstood.

Another quotation, from the great speech of Senator Jones:

GOLD THE CHEAPEST OF ALL THINGS.

There is no demand for gold in this country beyond the small amount necessary to pay the duties on imports and the interest on the national debt. When I come here from Nevada with gold and silver—the only money in circulation there—and find that it is too low in price, I cannot help it. In order to get its full value I must engage in foreign trade, become a gambler in the gold-room, or leave this country and go to France, England, or some other country where gold is the standard and circulates at its full value. If I stay here I must trade it for paper at a premium of 10 or 12 per cent. which, as I said before, is much less than the difference between paper and every other commodity. I have no remedy. I must submit to the loss. It is to the interest of this country that the real depreciation of paper should be exactly measured by the premium on gold.

If this extract shall not show the Hon. Senator's lack of comprehension of the subject, so pertinaciously discussed by him, the little we have to offer, may prove unavailing. He seems not to know, that there is a demand for gold, to meet the differences of exchange, which has so long existed against the nation. He seems to forget that fifty to one hundred millions besides, are required to meet the expenditures of the *pilgrim horde*, who visit Palestine and the Holy Land every year.

He seems not to know of the enormous sum of interest due annually and semi-annually, upon our railroad bonds held in Europe, and that the aggregate of these, added to sums he has had the grace to name, forms in itself the overwhelmning argument, against the views and policy enunciated by him. The miserly drivel, and ridiculous complaint, made by the Hon. Senator at having to sell *his coin* at ten or twelve per cent. premium, or engage in traffic with France or England, become a *gambler*, or find a residence in some other country *where gold does not command a premium*, is sickening to one, at least, who has made this coast his home for a quarter of a century.

It is wonderful, under the circumstances, that the Senate did not at once grant the Hon. Senator, an indefinite leave of absence.

If you fix a time for resumption it will not be the Government alone that will resume; that will be the least and easiest part of it. Resumption will take place on the part of the people of the country. If the Secretary of the Treasury alone were to redeem, he would be a shining mark against whom all the banking-houses of the world could make their combinations, and Wall street could assist in the work. They could and would make corners on him in gold, but they could not make corners on forty millions of people.

This is an enunciation, made by the Hon. Senator, which requires elucidation. It appeared to him, evidently, a task of such magnitude, that he passed it by, and left an understanding of his process, to the inference of the dear public, who have applauded him. We, understand what he says, but fail to comprehend fully and reliably, what he means.

SELL IF YOU NEED MONEY.

Loans on uncultivated lands have never been considered very desirable investments, more than upon salubrious climate or unutilized water courses. The long loans which are required to enable well-applied industry to anticipate at times the product of its fields would never be extended by the banks of circulation now asked for. These must come from saving banks, which require no charter from Government, but are the outgrowth of an industrious and commercial people. The land-owners of the South, though they fully realize that slavery is abolished, do not yet appreciate the new requirements of the great change in their industrial system. They have yet to learn that land alone is not productive enough to pay interest on nearly its value, besides wages and profits. The farmer must absolutely own the land he cultivates, and must not be at the mercy of money lenders. His true way to get money is by the sale of so much of his land as will enable him profitably to cultivate what is left. What avails it for the owner of two or three thousand acres of land to do nothing and say, "Well, it is a singular thing we have not more money; we ought to have more money, because we want to hire somebody to work, and we want the money to use as capital." If they want money very badly, they should as I have said, sell some of their land. Let them sell at the present prices, if they can; if they cannot, they should reduce the prices until somebody besides themselves shall see that it is a good bargain and be induced to buy. That is the way they do the world over.

The refusal of men with money to buy property at the extravagant estimate of its value by the owner is no evidence of hard times or of the scarcity of money. Money is plenty enough to buy things at their actual value, but the buyer must have something to say about the price he will give. It really seems childish for people to hold on convulsively to land and other property at double price, and then wonder that with them money is scarce and hard to be obtained. Money would have to be plentiful, indeed, and correspondingly cheap and worthless, if sellers were alone to fix the amount they should receive; that is to say, if the man with something to sell were to make the bargains for both sides. That is what is the matter in this country to-day. You have property inflated to a tremendous pitch, and the cry that comes here for more money means about this: "We are worth so much property; our land is worth so much, and we know it; but we cannot find anybody with money who is foolish enough to give us our price." Come down with your prices and you will find plenty of money. You never will find anybody with money who will give it to you. The man who would be willing to give present prices for property would not have any money long. He would soon get rid of it.

What say you of the East, the South, and the wide spead midland of the Republic, and you of the sunset-land, whose homes are planted on its western verge—whose hamlets front, and overlook the breaking waves of ocean at your feet, humble, hopeful toilers, that you are, striving to wrest from the mother earth, *that* which too many of her children seek to wrest from you. You, who risk more every year, of the capital and nerve at your command, than justice would apportion—reduced mayhap, by failing crops—by casualties of fire or flood—by sickness and by death—by unscrupulous and overreaching sharpers—by lying and undermining knaves, who hold a lien upon your homes, and threaten to foreclose, and turn you out again upon the world, or bind you in rental tribute, to their avarice and lust.

You farmers, of the Republic, who strive so patiently to rise above dependence, how like you this *counsel from the Senate?* This unfeeling slur upon your misfortunes? This cold rebuke and flippant insult to your manhood? This meddlesome and mercenary mockery of your distresses?

How like you the Hon. Senator's instructions in the management of your own affairs? His *scheme* to mend your finances? His attack upon your valuations of property without knowing whereof he speaks? His sweeping declarations, unconfined to any State—himself no purchaser, and therefore without venal inducement, even to beat you down, or to undervalue that you have to sell? Are you not ready to declare that the statesman, who travels in such paths as these, deserves the execration of high minded men?

Speaking of the balance of trade, the Hon. Senator says:

The balance of trade is never against me, because I do not buy anything I do not want, and never pay anything more for a thing than I think it is worth. Therefore the trade is just even. I really think I have a little the best of it.

The complacency of this boast is in admirable keeping with the impressive personality of the speaker. His attempt to illustrate the important subject of "the balance of trade" by reference to himself and his manner of dealing, may provoke a smile, even on the part of those who are acquainted with his *resources*. It is clear that the Hon. Senator has not studied that branch of logic which teaches the rules and modes of reasoning.

Another extract being in order, we will say that it is the last, save one, which has been considered worthy of reference to in this examination. He says:

A state of profound peace has reigned for nearly ten years throughout the land with no immediate menace of war. With a climate and soil unsurpased, with a population as enterprising, industrious and ingenious as any upon the face of the earth, we see to-day, instead of the prosperity which these conditions commonly insure, the industries of the country paralyzed, trade stagnant and distrust prevailing everywhere. The cause for this can be found nowhere except in the inferior and vicious agent used for stimulating the industries, effecting the exchanges, and distributing the wealth of the country.

What can the Hon. Senator offer to controvert a fact, that for and during nine years of the time he names, the prosperity of the country was the most marked and absolute, considering its status at close of the war, that has ever been known to us. Only since the panic have the Bullionists had anything to bark at; and now, working in the interest of the money rings of the country, they try to make it appear that the country is ruined by a Government substitute for gold, *without which*, worse than the paralysis referred to by Senator Jones, would have characterized the condition of the country since the close of the war.

If greenbacks sustained the industries and the credit of the country when it contained not more than 200 millions of gold (and *that* mortgaged to Europe), what shall oppose our faith and acceptance of it now, while the drain of gold permits no increase of it, as a circulating medium.

To denominate the national currency, "the vicious agent" used for stimulating industries, is to oppose industry, and no Senator can be upheld in such a course

At nearly the close of his speech, the Hon. Senator says:

I have neither time or inclination to make comparative estimates of the amount of money in circulation per capita in this and other commercial countries. There can be no doubt that we have a redundancy of it whenever the market price of gold is above its Mint price.

Again, do we find occasion for insisting *that the general, or ruling rate of interest for money, is the measure of its supply, and the only lawful evidence of abundance.* Was money abundant in New York and the Eastern cities not long ago, when it commanded one and sometimes two per cent. per day interest.

Does the Hon. Senator mean to have us understand that money capable of being so controlled and cornered, is abundant? Does he mean to go further and insist that there was at that time a redundancy? If he does, it will be a gain to the people when money shall be so plenty that three per cent. per annum shall become the rule, and not the exception, and so distributed that Wall street can no more control it to their especial gain, than the *air* which is and ever should be, free to all.

In 1749, England was enabled to reduce her rates of interest (not on her indebtness, but to her industries) to three per cent. per annum, and by the efforts of the Government to keep it there, has done more to stimulate industry and enterprise than any nation on earth.

It would be well for this Government to follow, for the benefit which may come to us, the policy which England has so wisely adopted for the advancement of her national concerns.

It is by the abundance of money, no matter of what description, if it be good, and carries on its face the stamp and approval of the Government, that our resources can be developed and utilized, our enterprise stimulated, and our industrious arms supported and encouraged. Whosoever, opposes these beneficent provisions, himself convicts of wrong, and must suffer the condemnation of an outraged and too confiding people.

We know not Senator Jones, personally. From the reputation which he bore among men, we thought him more liberal and intelligent. We expected to have been instructed by his knowledge, and enlivened by the vivid splendor of his eloquence. We confess to a disappointment that makes us incisively inclined. Our disappointment is intensified, by observing that the Press of the Pacific Coast, and many in the East, whom we have looked to for an intelligent interpretation of truth and right, have set the seal of greatness on this speech of Senator Jones, and made him appear the peer of any man that lives. Henceforth, the irreverent pillars of the Democracy shall cease to exclaim, "*Jesus Christ*, and *General Jackson!*" and utilize the accredited syllepsis of "Jesus Christ and John P. Jones" !!! A renown that is acquired by an assault on the beneficent measures of the Government—and the estimable men who introduced and supported them, and by *ad captandum* appeals to the prejudices of the vicious and the ignorant—stands so near to execrable notoriety, that he who wins it may wear it if he can.

The analyses of infected air is not a pleasant task, and we shall conclude with the announcement of our own opinion of the great speech of Senator Jones, that it is a paraphrase of the Antique Liturgy of the Democratic Political Economists, imponderable as smoke, as capable of compression, and as inexpensive as the ammunition of an air gun.

San Francisco, June, 1874.

www.ingramcontent.com/pod-product-compliance
Lightning Source LLC
LaVergne TN
LVHW011138110826
845150LV00008B/2384
* 9 7 8 1 4 1 8 1 9 3 6 5 2 *